Easy To Make And Use

WINTER BULLETIN BOARDS

by
Imogene Forte

Incentive Publications, Inc.
Nashville, Tennessee

Edited by Sally Sharpe
Bulletin boards illustrated by Marta Zellars
Cover by Susan Eaddy

ISBN 0-86530-168-9

Copyright © 1987 by Incentive Publications, Inc., Nashville, TN. All rights reserved. Permission is hereby granted to the purchaser of one copy of Winter Bulletin Boards to reproduce, in sufficient quantity to meet the needs of students in one classroom, pages bearing the following statement:
© 1987 by Incentive Publications, Inc., Nashville, TN. All rights reserved.

Table of Contents

About This Book v

Special Ways To Use The Winter Letter Patterns vi

Handy Rules For Winter Safety 7
    Patterns: Left And Right Hands Wearing
           Gloves, Snowflakes

Winter Cinquains 10

Snowing All About Compound Words 11
    Patterns: Two Snowmen

Tree-mendous Work 13
    Pattern: Tree

Rock Into The Holidays 15
    Pattern: Rocking Horse

Holidays Are Happier With Good Books 17
    Patterns: Candle, Tree, Reindeer, Star

Aloha! Winter Brings Sunshine, Not Snow 20
    Patterns: Hula Dancer, Palm Tree, Coconuts

Christmas Under Sunny Skies 23
    Pattern: Skinny Santa Wearing Swimming Trunks

Ho! Ho! Ho! 25
    Pattern: Santa Holding Sack

Wishing You A Purr-fect Christmas 27
    Patterns: Two Cats Wearing Stocking Caps,
        Two Bows

Dizzy Dreidel 30
    Pattern: Dreidel

Sing A Song Of Chanukah 32
    Patterns: Four Hebrew Letters, Musical Notes

"No Lion", We Will Keep Our Resolutions 35
    Pattern: Lion

An Idea A Day Keeps Boredom Away 37
    Pattern: Light Bulb

Be My Funny Valentine 39
    Patterns: Three Hearts

Healthy Hearts Are Happy Hearts 41
    Patterns: Four Hearts With Smiling Faces,
        Human Heart

A Letter Is Better 44

Splash Heard Around The World 45
    Pattern: Space Capsule With Astronaut

Winter Is Sliding Into Spring 47
    Patterns: Sled, Boy, Melting Snowman

Winter Letter Patterns 51

ABOUT THIS BOOK

Brighten up your classroom and help "stamp out" the winter blahs with these topically-themed bulletin boards. Designed with the busy teacher in mind, this book contains over 24 bulletin boards complete with patterns, suggested materials, construction suggestions, activities, and additional captions and ideas.

Over 30 patterns have been included to make the construction of the boards easy and quick. When larger displays are needed, simply enlarge the patterns by using an opaque projector or by drawing them free-hand. The patterns can also be reproduced for your students to use in helping construct the boards or for additional art and study projects. An extra feature is the inclusion of 26 winter letter patterns which may be used with the boards or in many other creative ways (see the next page for more details).

These boards have been designed to add color and excitement to your classroom and to involve your students in fun learning activities all winter long!

SPECIAL WAYS TO USE THE WINTER LETTER PATTERNS

Create beautiful bulletin boards and banners and excite your students with letter projects and games with the 26 winter letter patterns in this book!

CONSTRUCTION

An easy way to cut out the letters is to reproduce a letter page, mount the page on construction paper (spray adhesive works well), and cut the page into quarters. For convenience and versatility, make four copies of the letters A, E, I, and O, three copies of N, R, S, and T, two copies of F, L, M, P, and U, and one copy each of the remaining letters. Have students color the letters or color them yourself. You may also cut around each letter individually to achieve a different look. Any way you choose to cut, color, or mount the letters, your "always-on-hand" alphabet will make eye-catching bulletin boards and displays every time!

PROJECTS

- String the letters with yarn to make a banner for a chalkboard or door.

- Let students color the letters and string them together to make a special message for a friend or relative.

- String the letters "VIP" together and hang them around the neck of a student deserving special recognition.

- Give each student a letter and ask him or her to write a story about the character on the letter.

- Give each student the letters in his or her name. Ask each student to write a story about the scenes portrayed on the letters.

Knot the yarn to keep the letters in place

GAMES

Give each student a letter to wear around his or her neck.

- Randomly call groups to the front of the class and have them arrange themselves alphabetically. (This is good for young children who are working on alphabetical skills.)

- Call a group of approximately ten students to the front of the class. Ask the other students in the class to make a word find puzzle using the letters represented in the group.

- Having a particular word in mind, call students to the front of the class who are wearing the letters in the chosen word. Be sure to randomly call them forward. Have the other students unscramble the letters to spell the word.

SUGGESTED MATERIALS
- blue background
- white snowflakes
- white rectangular cards
- white caption and border
- construction-paper hands

CONSTRUCTION
Enlarge the hand patterns and color them with markers or cut them out of construction paper of the desired color. Instruct students to trace and cut out their own hand patterns. Attach snowflakes to the board.

USE
Discuss winter safety rules. Write several rules on rectangular cards and attach them to the childrens' hand patterns on the board as shown. Review the rules regularly and substitute new ones periodically.

SUGGESTED MATERIALS
- dark blue background
- white paper for cinquain model
- construction-paper winter objects
- white caption

CONSTRUCTION
Make a large cinquain poem model for the board. Use the above poem or substitute one of your own.

USE
Discuss cinquains and provide the class with several examples. Have students make winter objects using the patterns throughout this book (snowman, snowflake, sled, candle, etc.). Ask each student to write an original cinquain on a winter object. Display the poems on the board.

SUGGESTED MATERIALS
- blue background
- white caption and border
- white snowmen
- white pockets
- pipe cleaners for arms
- small tagboard snowmen

CONSTRUCTION
Enlarge the snowmen. Color the features with markers and make arms with pipe cleaners. Reproduce the patterns to make several small snowmen. Cut the snowmen out of tagboard. Use a black marker to write a compound word on the front of each snowman and duplicate numbers on the back as shown on page 12. Cut each snowman in half. Make two sturdy pockets to hold the top and bottom halves of the snowmen.

USE
Allow a pair of students to take the snowmen halves out of the pockets and lay them on a nearby table. Instruct the students to make compound words. If the numbers on the back of a snowman match, the compound word is correct.

ADDITIONAL BOARDS
SNOWING ALL ABOUT CONTRACTIONS
SNOWING ALL ABOUT HOMONYMS

SUGGESTED MATERIALS
- white or light blue background
- red caption and border
- green trees
- materials for trimming (tissue paper, beads, fabric scraps, foil, etc.)

CONSTRUCTION
Let each student decorate a tree for the board. Students may wish to use squares of tissue paper to decorate their trees as shown on page 14.

USE
Display original stories and poems or excellent tests and papers on the trees.

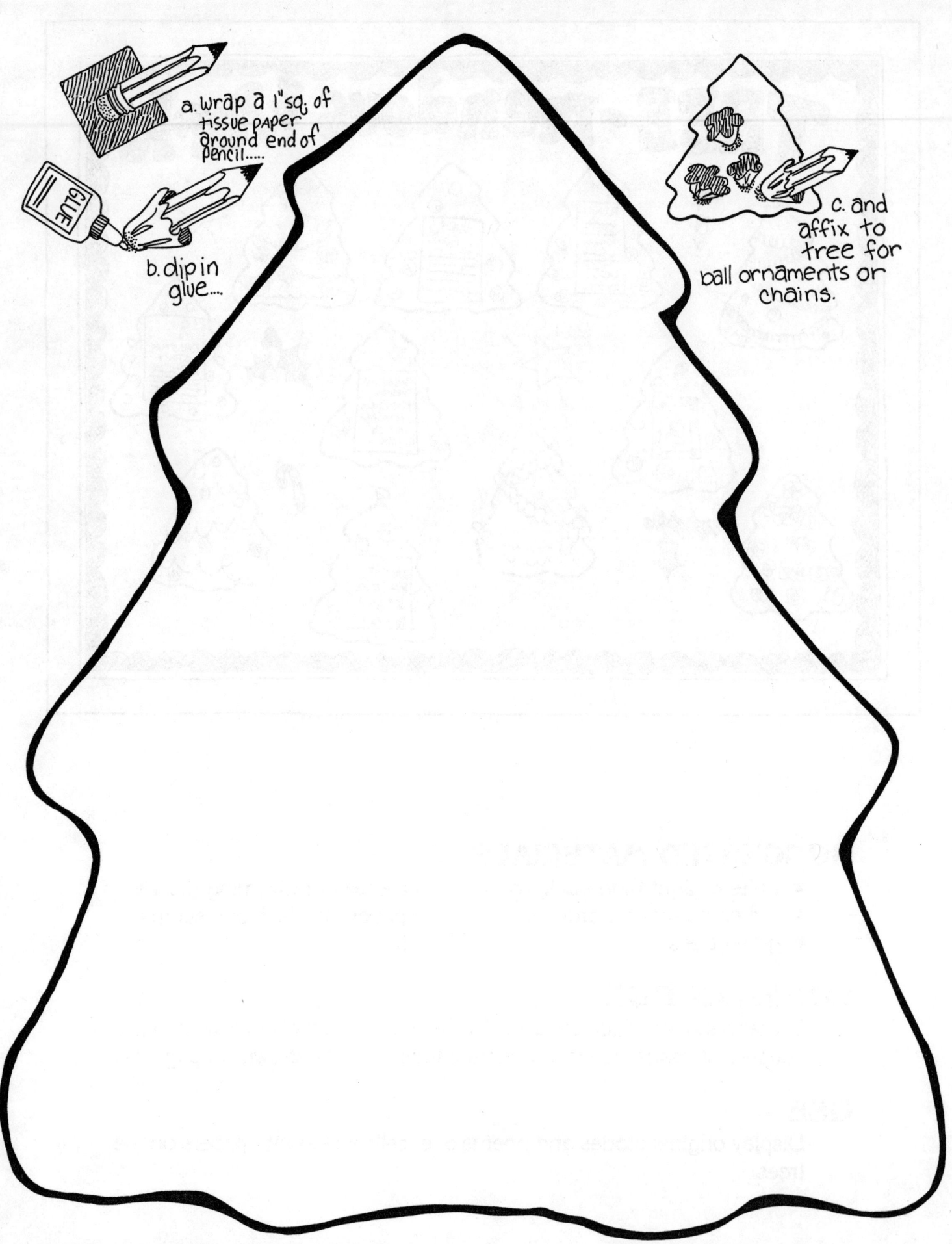

SUGGESTED MATERIALS
- blue background
- red caption
- white horse
- string for reins

CONSTRUCTION
Enlarge the rocking horse pattern. Cut a horse out of white construction paper and color features with markers.

USE
Have students use construction paper to create colorful objects which remind them of winter holidays (skis, sleds, ice skates, candy canes, presents, trees, musical notes, cookies, etc.). Use the board as a showplace for holiday art.

ADDITIONAL BOARDS
ROCK INTO GOOD WORK
GOOD DEEDS, HAPPY THOUGHTS
HOLIDAY FUN

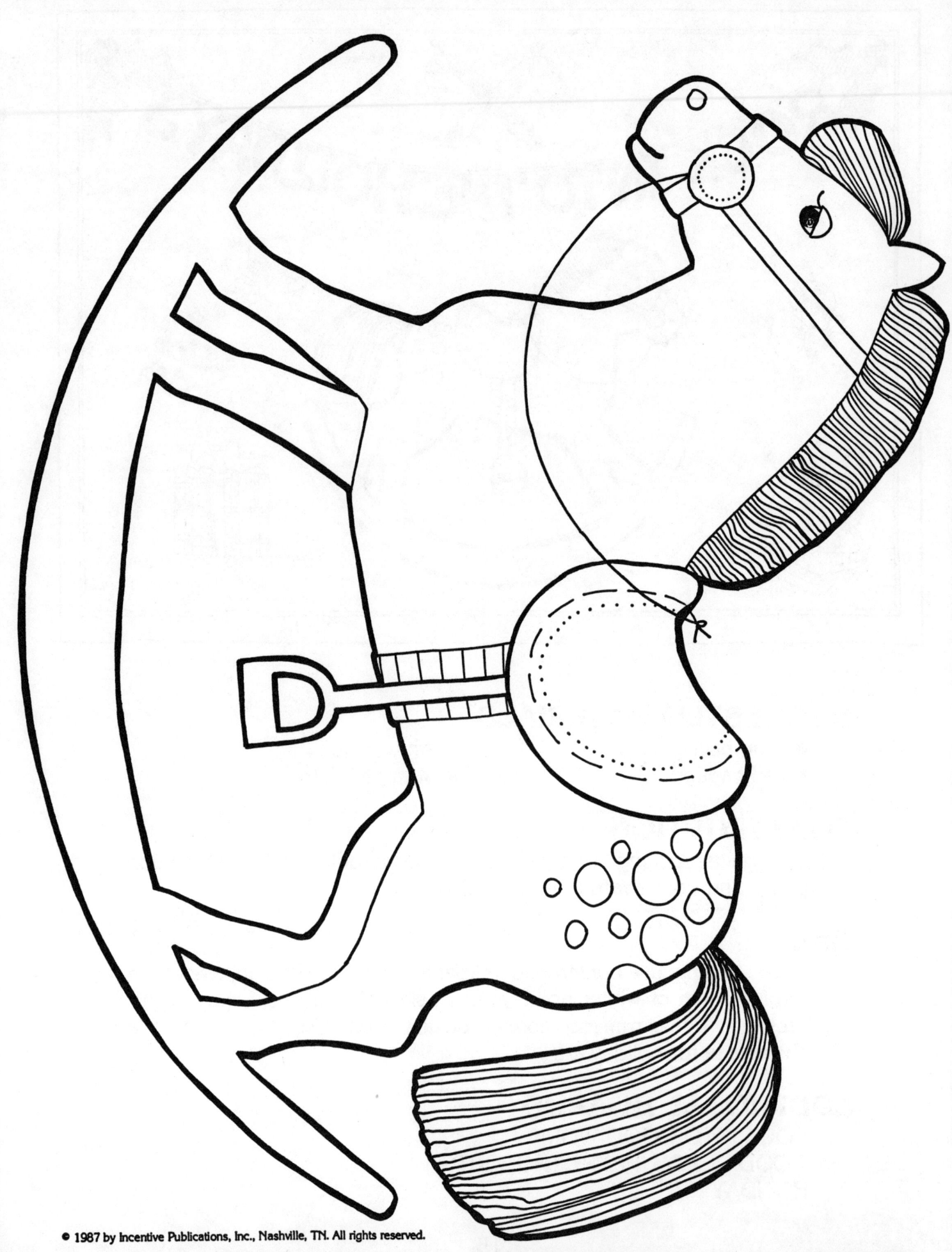

SUGGESTED MATERIALS
- red background
- green caption
- green trees
- brown reindeer
- yellow candles

CONSTRUCTION
Have students cut out and decorate the patterns. Ask each student to write the name of a favorite book, its author, and his or her own name on a pattern.

ADDITIONAL BOARDS
HOLIDAYS AROUND THE WORLD: Have students write ways that Christmas is celebrated in other countries on the patterns.
CHRISTMAS IS A DEER TIME: Have each student write his or her name on a reindeer pattern. Display the deer on the board.
THESE LITTLE DEERS WISH YOU A MERRY CHRISTMAS: Display students' reindeer on the board.

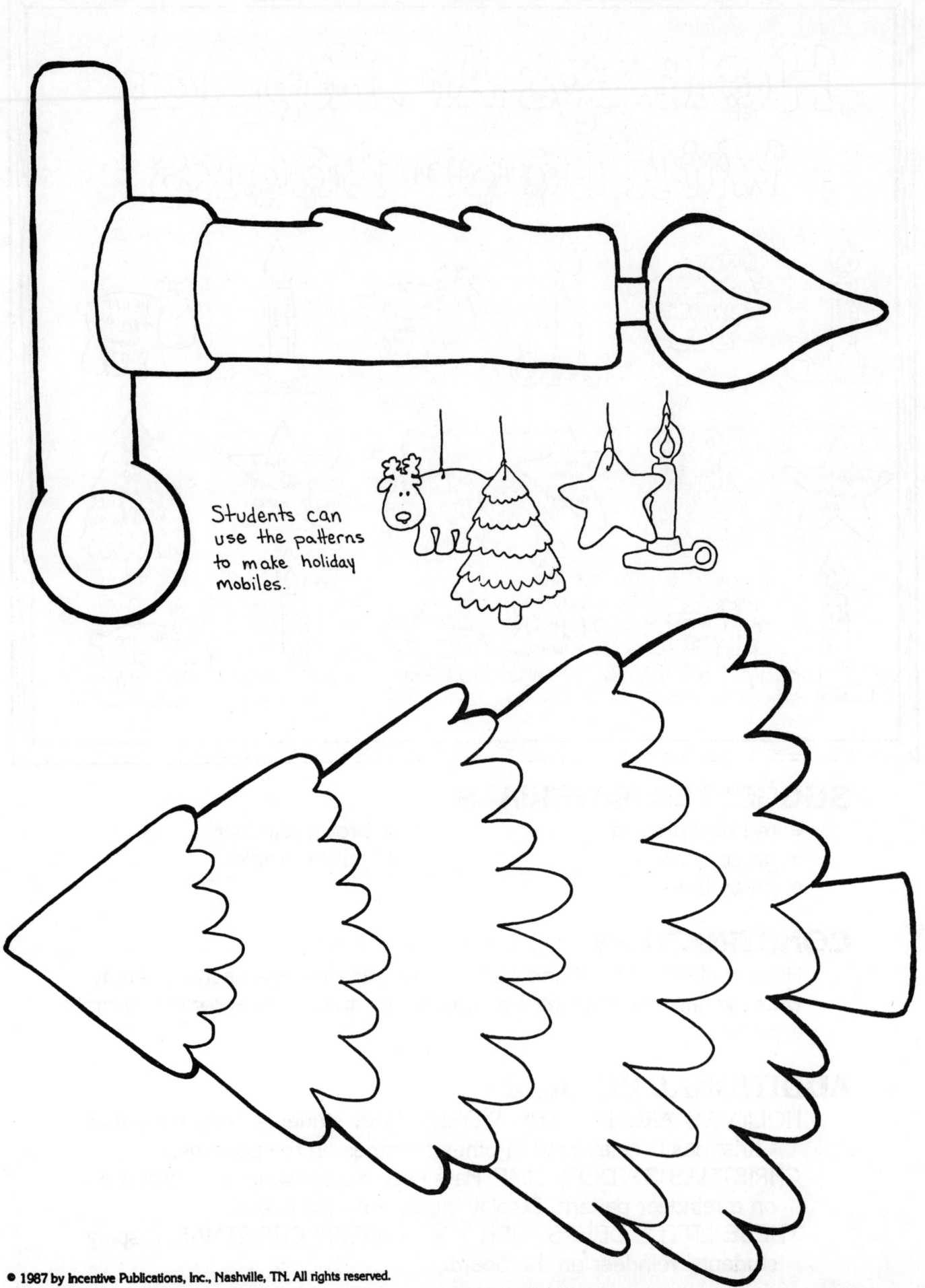

Students can use the patterns to make holiday mobiles.

Use star or reindeer pattern as name or gift tags, or for party invitations.

SUGGESTED MATERIALS
- light blue sky
- green grass
- white clouds
- yellow sun
- green palm tree, brown trunk
- brown coconuts
- white caption

USE
Discuss parts of the world that are warm all year long and never have snow or ice. Have students research and write reports about such places. Display the reports on the board.

SUGGESTED MATERIALS
- light blue sky
- green grass
- white clouds
- yellow sun
- white caption
- green palm tree, brown trunk
- brown coconuts
- colorful lanterns
- construction-paper packages

CONSTRUCTION
Use the pattern on page 22 to make a palm tree. Use construction paper to make colorful lanterns to hang from the tree. Have each student make a package for the board.

ADDITIONAL BOARDS
I'M DREAMING OF A SUNNY CHRISTMAS

ONCE UPON A CHRISTMAS: Have students write Christmas stories to be displayed on the board.

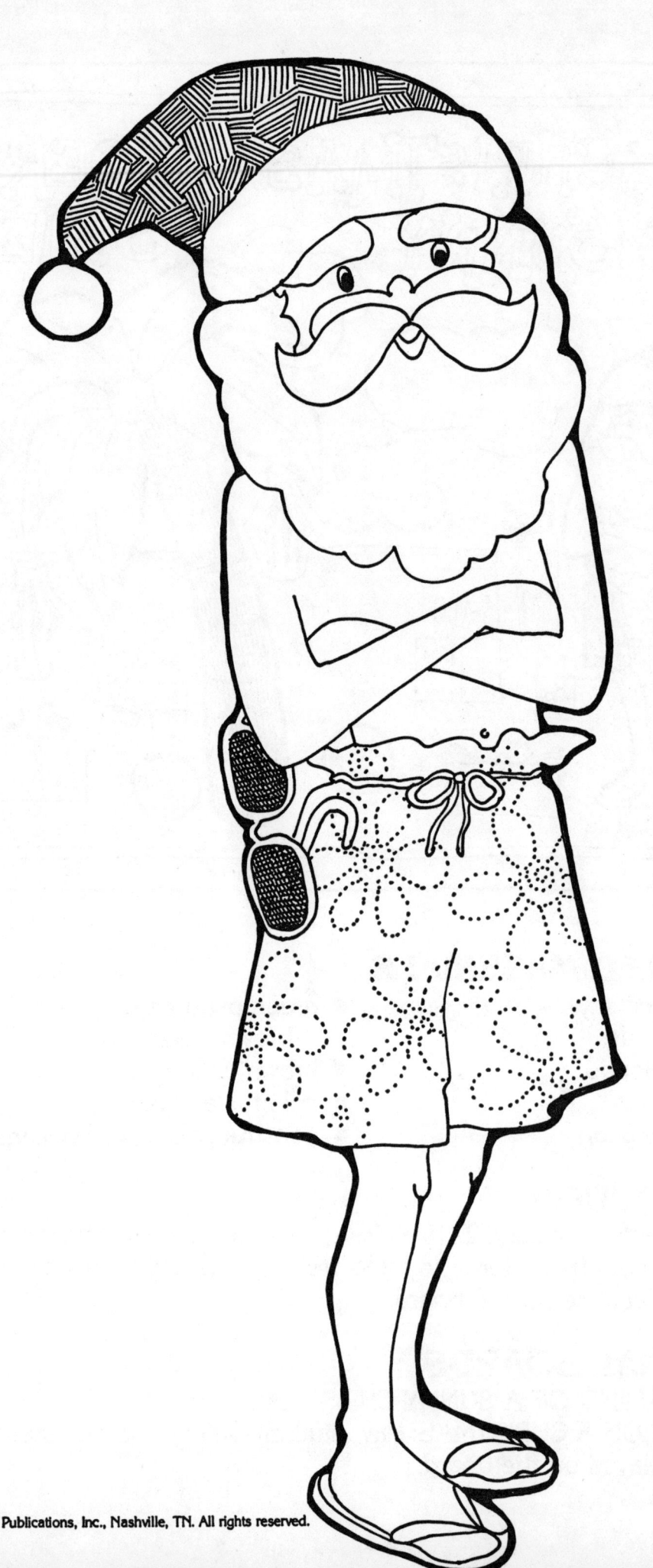

SUGGESTED MATERIALS
- green background
- white paper for Santa
- red caption
- cotton for Santa's suit

CONSTRUCTION
Enlarge the Santa pattern and color it with markers. Glue cotton to Santa's beard, eyelashes, and fur trim.

USE
Have students draw, color, and cut out pictures of what they would like for Christmas. Place the items in Santa's sack and around Santa's feet.

ADDITIONAL PATTERN USE
Use the Santa pattern to make tree or window decorations. Decorate the Santas with scraps of tissue paper, fabric, cotton, or markers. Punch a hole in the top and insert yarn to make a loop for hanging.

© 1987 by Incentive Publications, Inc., Nashville, TN. All rights reserved.

SUGGESTED MATERIALS
- green background
- silver or gold foil caption
- white kittens and caps
- sequins, buttons, scrap material
- pipe cleaners for whiskers

CONSTRUCTION
Use scrap materials or crayons and markers to decorate the kittens' stocking caps. Give the kittens colorful bow ties and pipe-cleaner whiskers. Have each student write a Christmas wish on the kittens' backs.

ADDITIONAL BOARDS
CHRISTMAS IS A PURR-FECT TIME TO SAY...
HAPPY NEW YEAR: Have students decorate the kittens' stocking caps for New Year's and write New Year wishes on the kittens' backs.

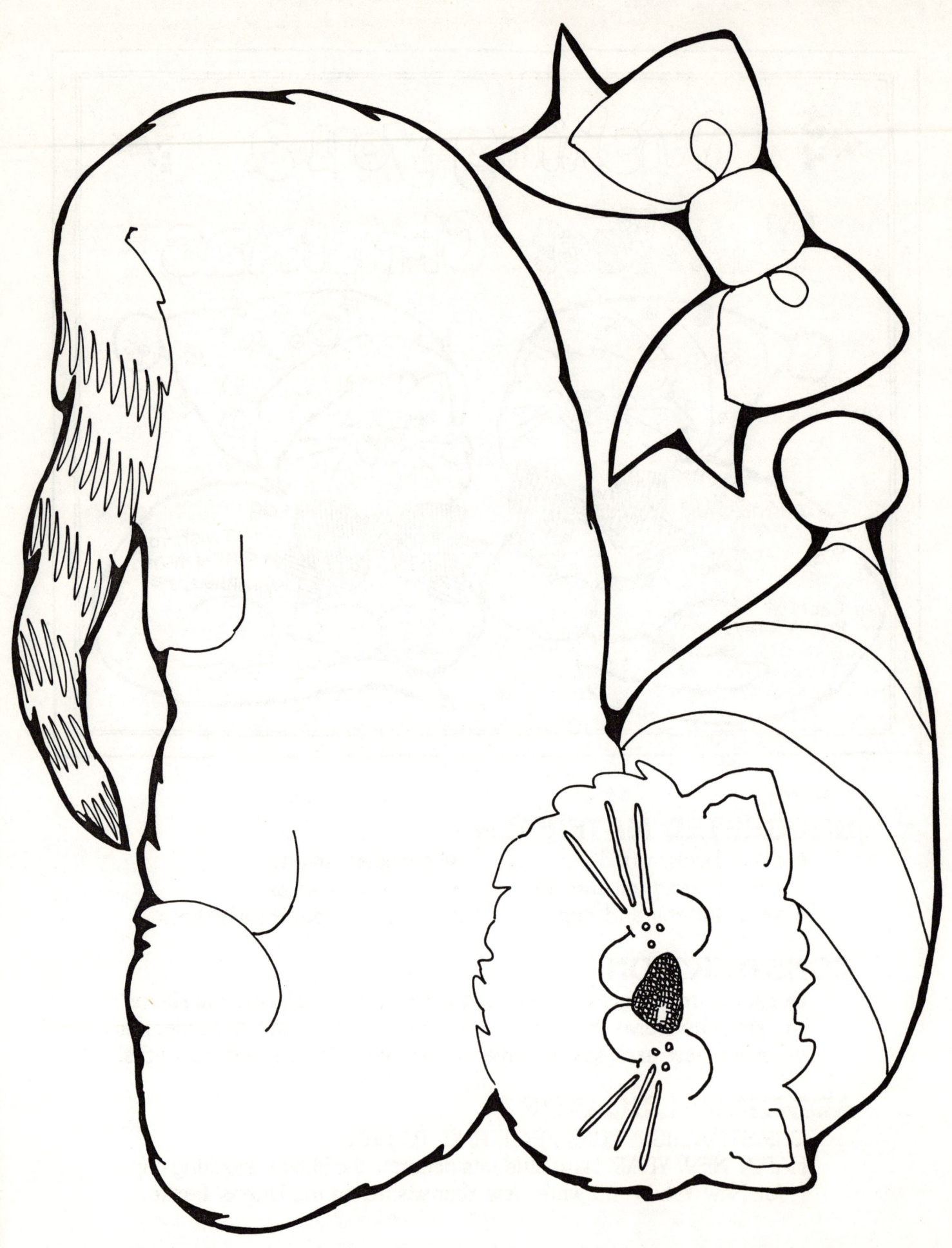

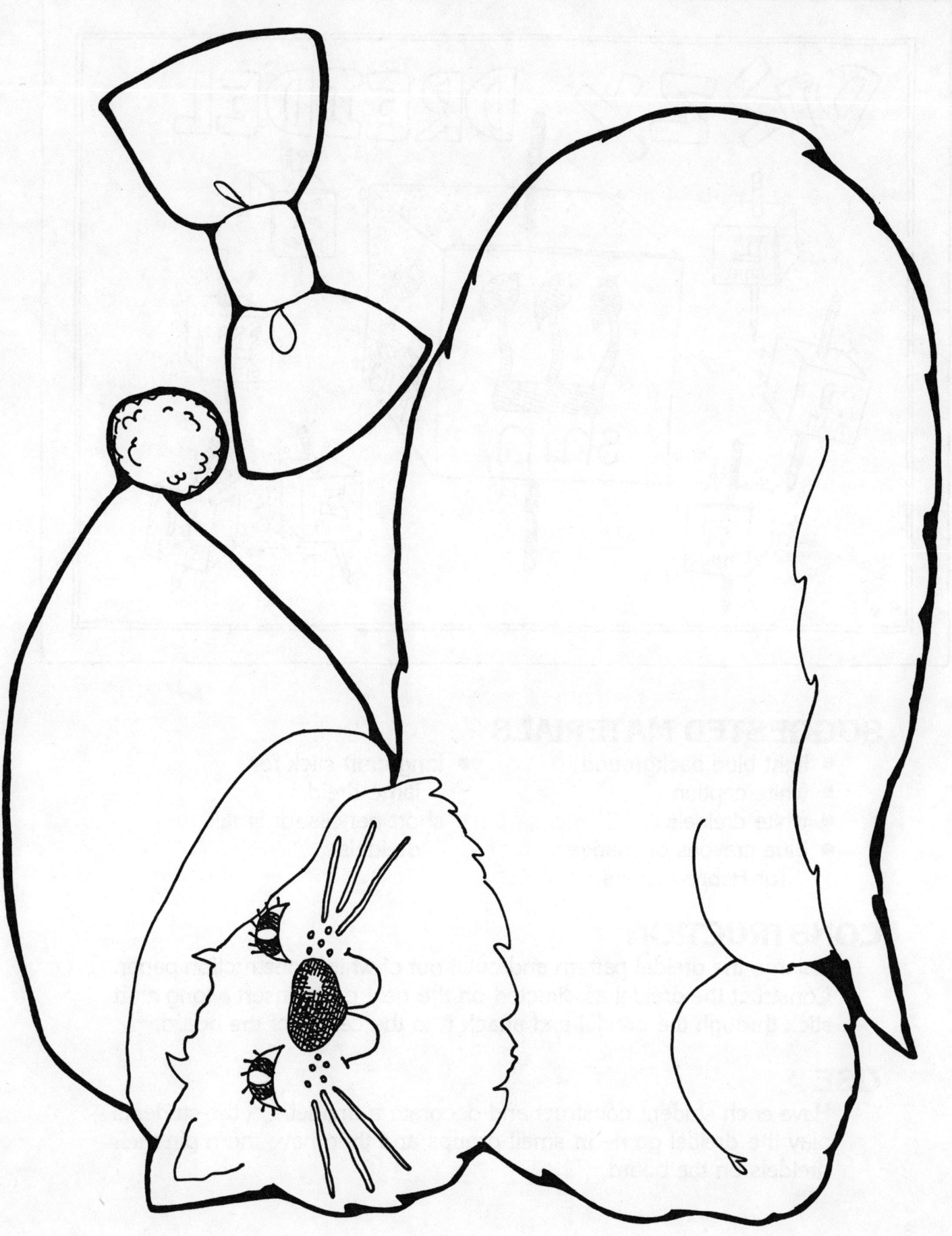

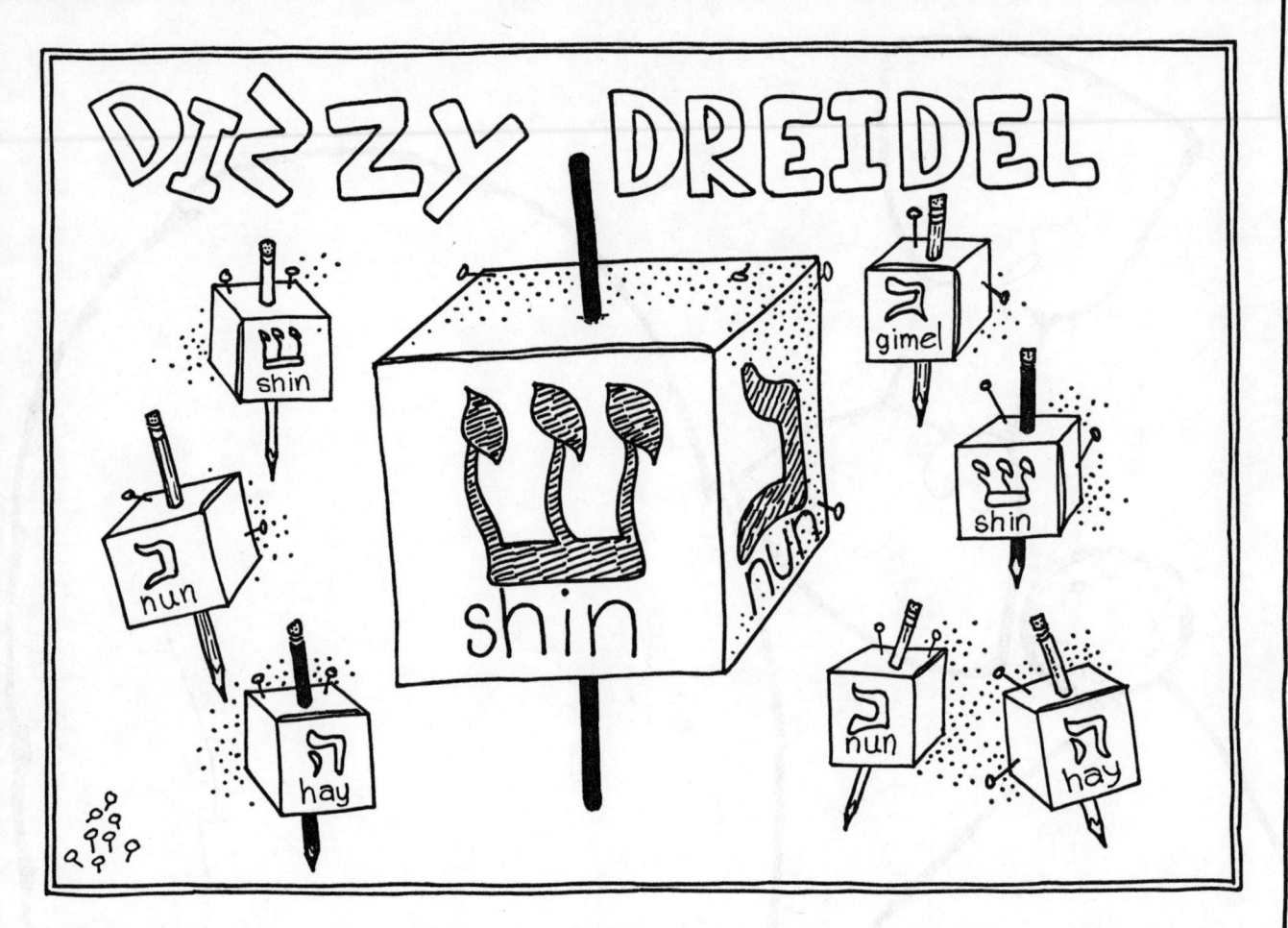

SUGGESTED MATERIALS
- light blue background
- white caption
- white dreidels
- blue crayons or markers for Hebrew letters
- long craft stick for large dreidel
- short pencils for small dreidels

CONSTRUCTION
Enlarge the dreidel pattern and cut it out of white construction paper. Construct the dreidel as directed on the next page. Insert a long craft stick through the dreidel and attach it to the center of the board.

USE
Have each student construct and decorate a dreidel. Let the students play the dreidel game in small groups and then have them pin their dreidels on the board.

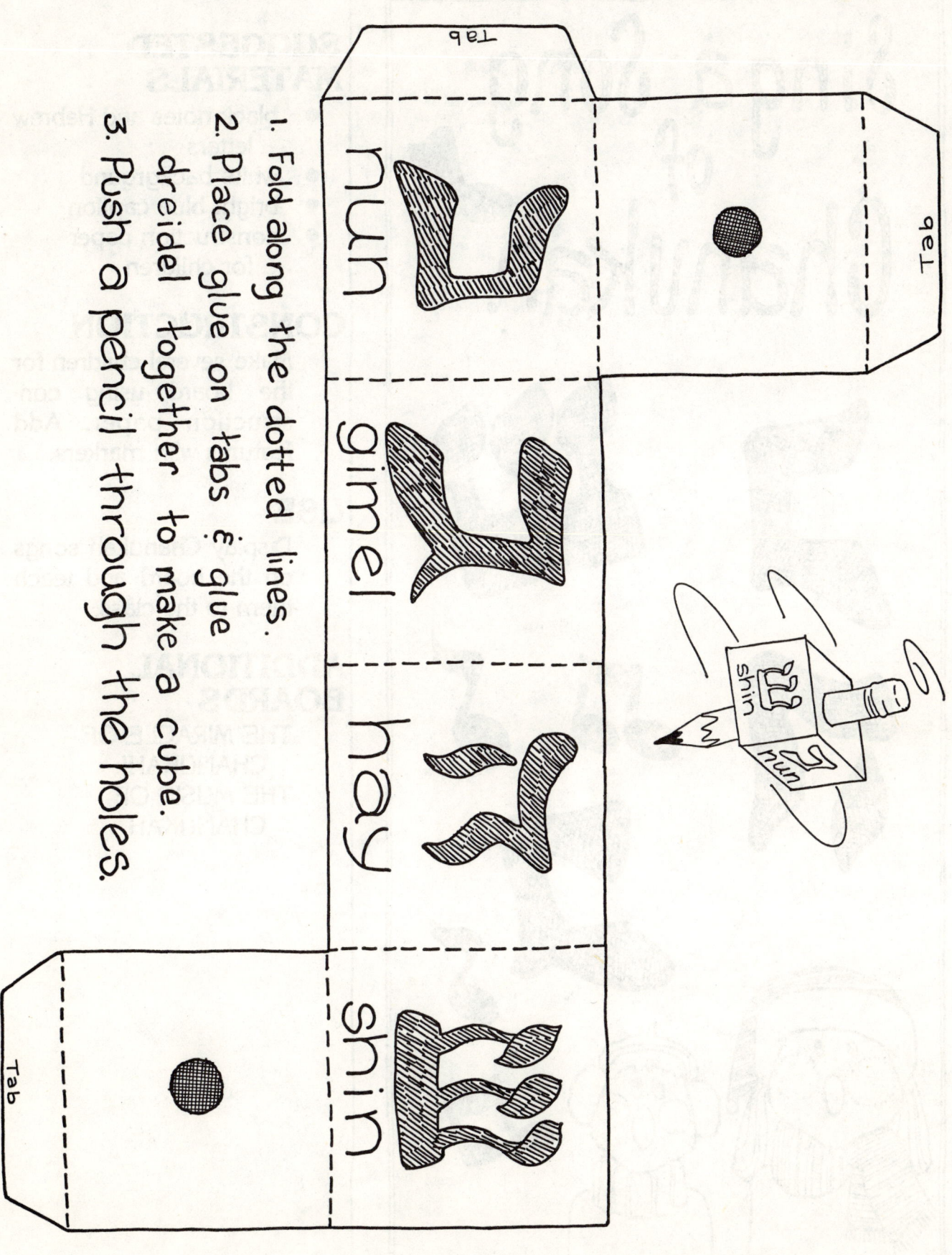

1. Fold along the dotted lines.
2. Place glue on tabs & glue dreidel together to make a cube.
3. Push a pencil through the holes.

© 1987 by Incentive Publications, Inc., Nashville, TN. All rights reserved.

Sing a Song of Chanukah

SUGGESTED MATERIALS
- black notes and Hebrew letters
- white background
- bright blue caption
- construction paper for children

CONSTRUCTION
Make several children for the board using construction paper. Add features with markers.

USE
Display Chanukah songs on the board and teach them to the class.

ADDITIONAL BOARDS
THE MIRACLE OF CHANUKAH!
THE MUSIC OF CHANUKAH

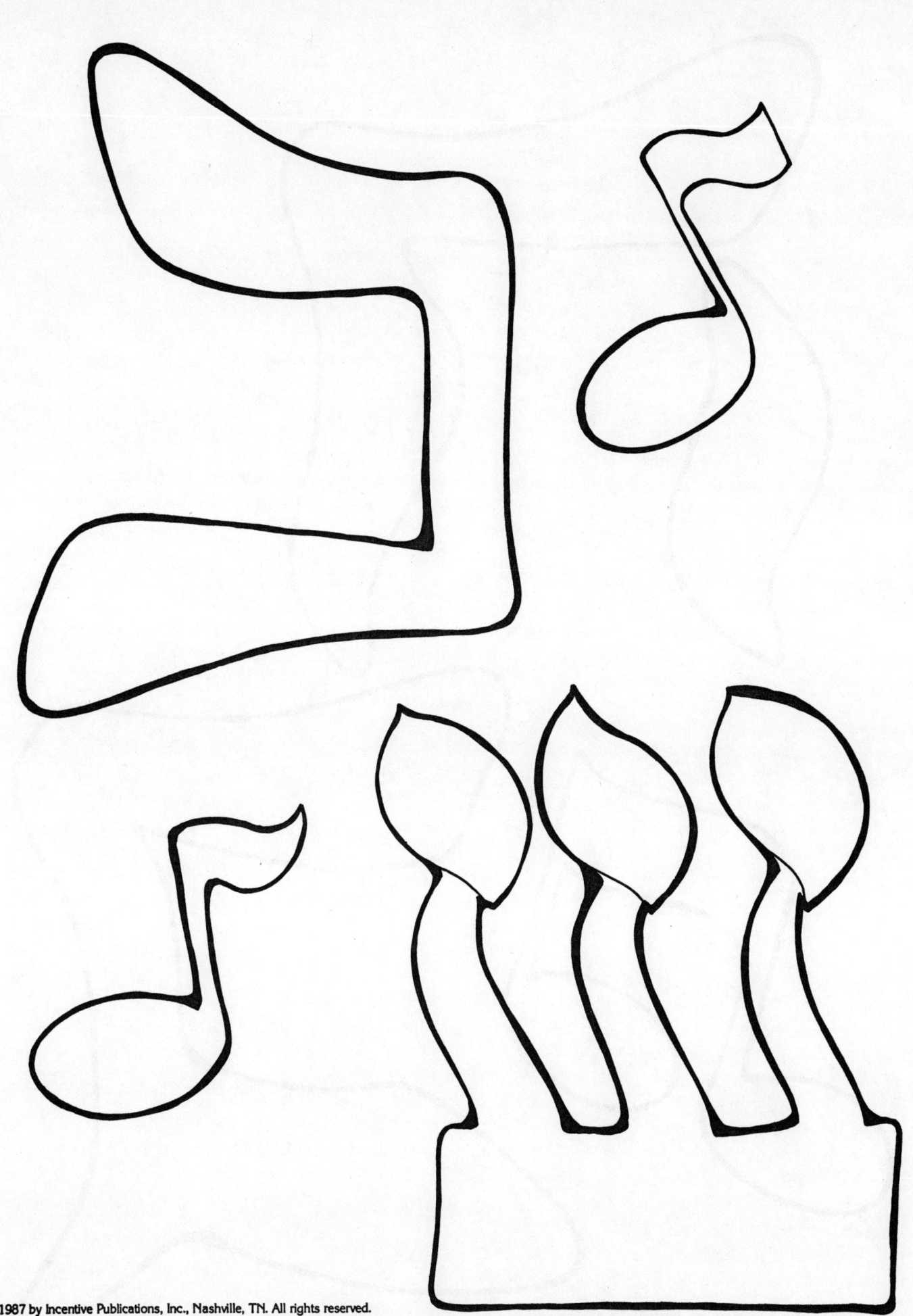

SUGGESTED MATERIALS
- yellow background
- black caption
- white "blurbs"
- pipe-cleaner whiskers
- brown lion

CONSTRUCTION
Have students write New Year's resolutions on white "blurbs" to attach to the board.

ADDITIONAL BOARDS
WINTER: IN LIKE A LION, OUT LIKE A LAMB
ROARING ABOUT GOOD WORK

SUGGESTED MATERIALS
- blue background
- yellow caption
- yellow strips for light rays
- white "blurbs"
- yellow light bulb

USE
Ask students to write ideas from which famous inventions resulted on white "blurbs".

ADDITIONAL BOARDS
A WEEK OF BRIGHT IDEAS
EDISON, GALILEO, NEWTON AND YOU

Note: National New Idea Week Februray 5-12

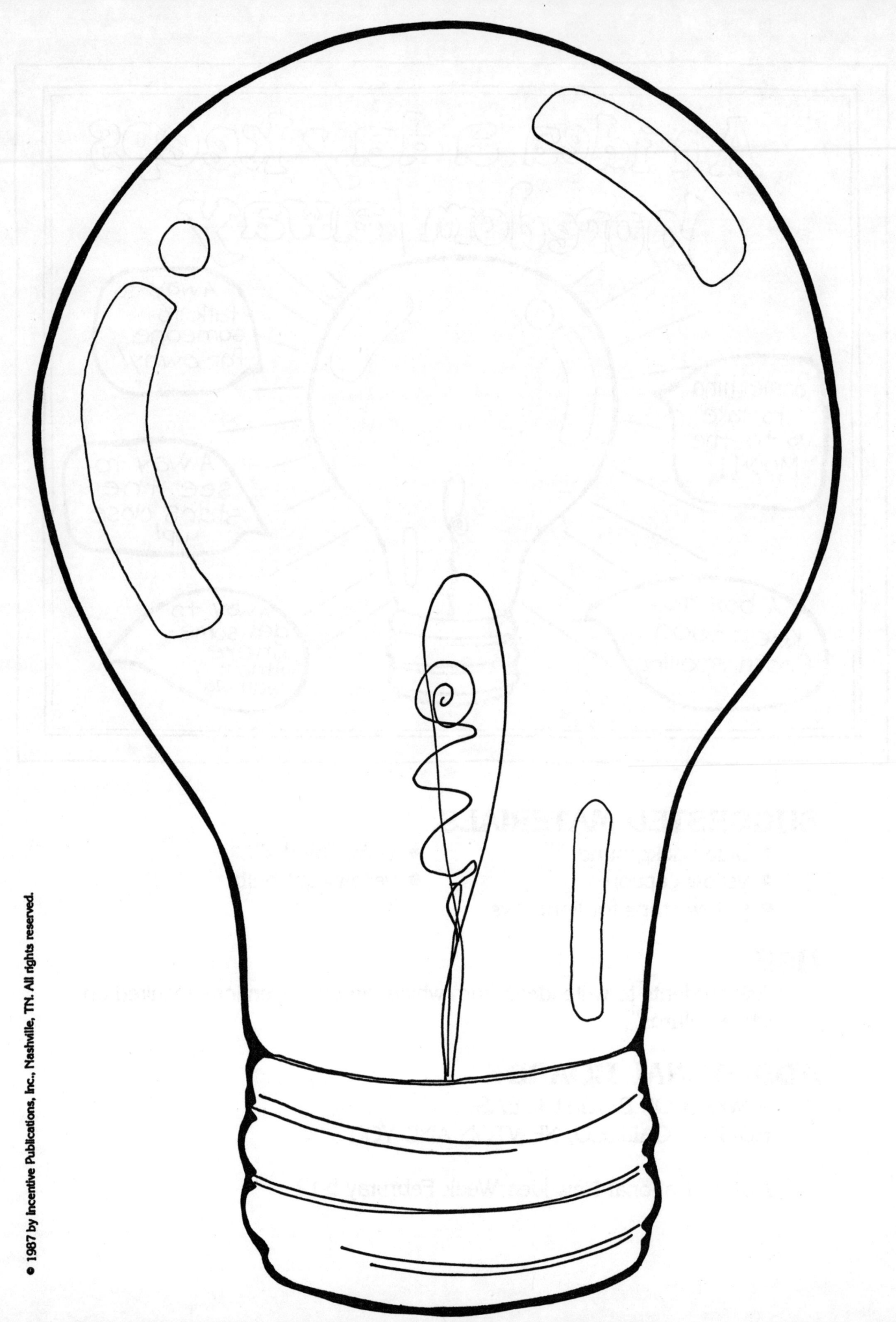

SUGGESTED MATERIALS
- colorful construction paper
- crayons and markers
- white background
- red or pink hearts
- red or pink caption

CONSTRUCTION
Have each student make a "funny valentine" animal or character. Arms and legs may be made from folded construction paper strips (see page 42). Students may add features with crayons and markers or construction paper.

USE
Ask each student to write a cartoon valentine message on his or her "funny valentine".

Note: Heart patterns on page 42 may be used also.

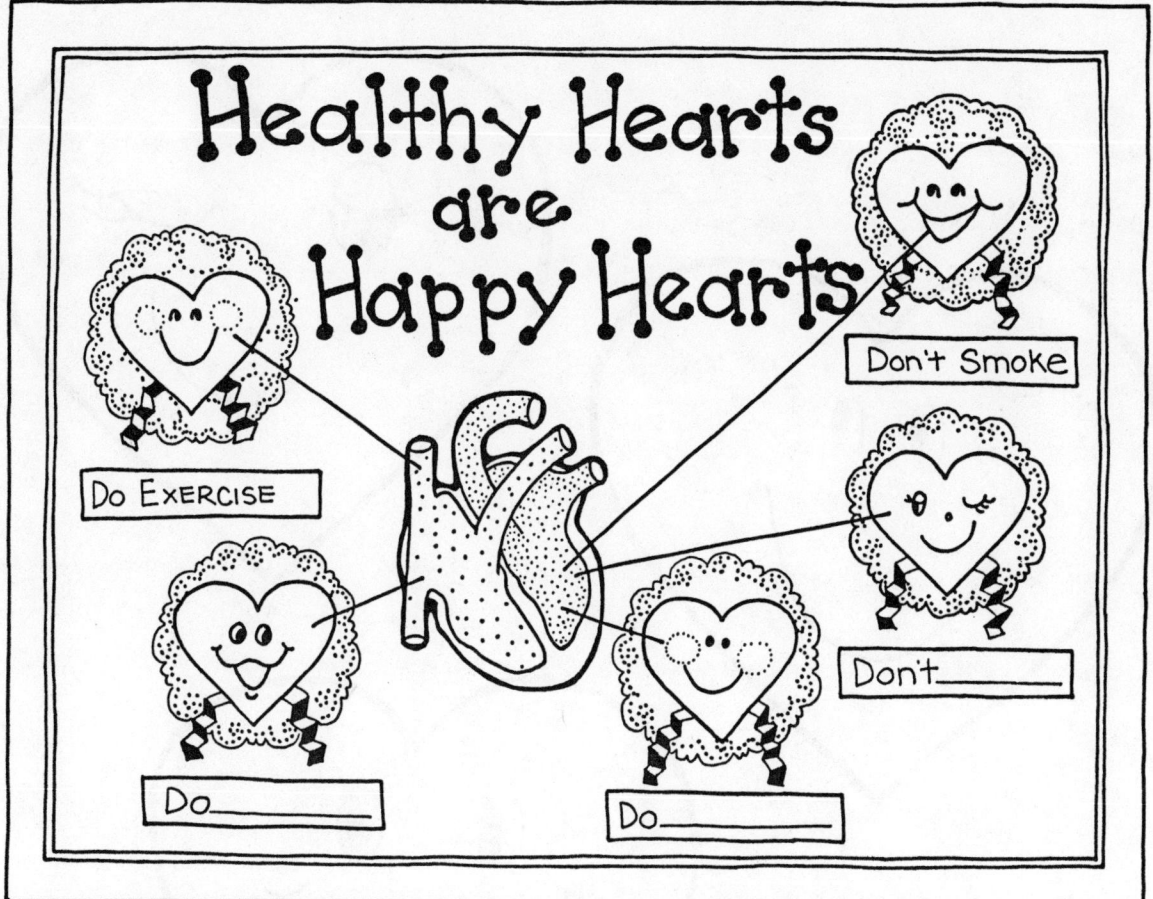

SUGGESTED MATERIALS
- white background
- pink or red caption
- pink or red hearts
- white human heart
- black strips for arms
- white rectangular cards
- white doilies
- red yarn

CONSTRUCTION
Use markers to color the human heart. Attach the heart to the center of the board. Decorate red smiling hearts with a black marker. Make "accordion" arms with black strips of construction paper. Glue the hearts to white doilies. Link the smiling hearts to the human heart with red yarn.

USE
Have the class research and discuss the human heart. Instruct students to write the "do's" and don't's" of maintaining a healthy heart on white rectangular cards. Attach the cards beneath the hearts as shown.

ADDITIONAL BOARD
HEARTWARMING EXPERIENCES: Display students' themes or original stories about heartwarming experiences.

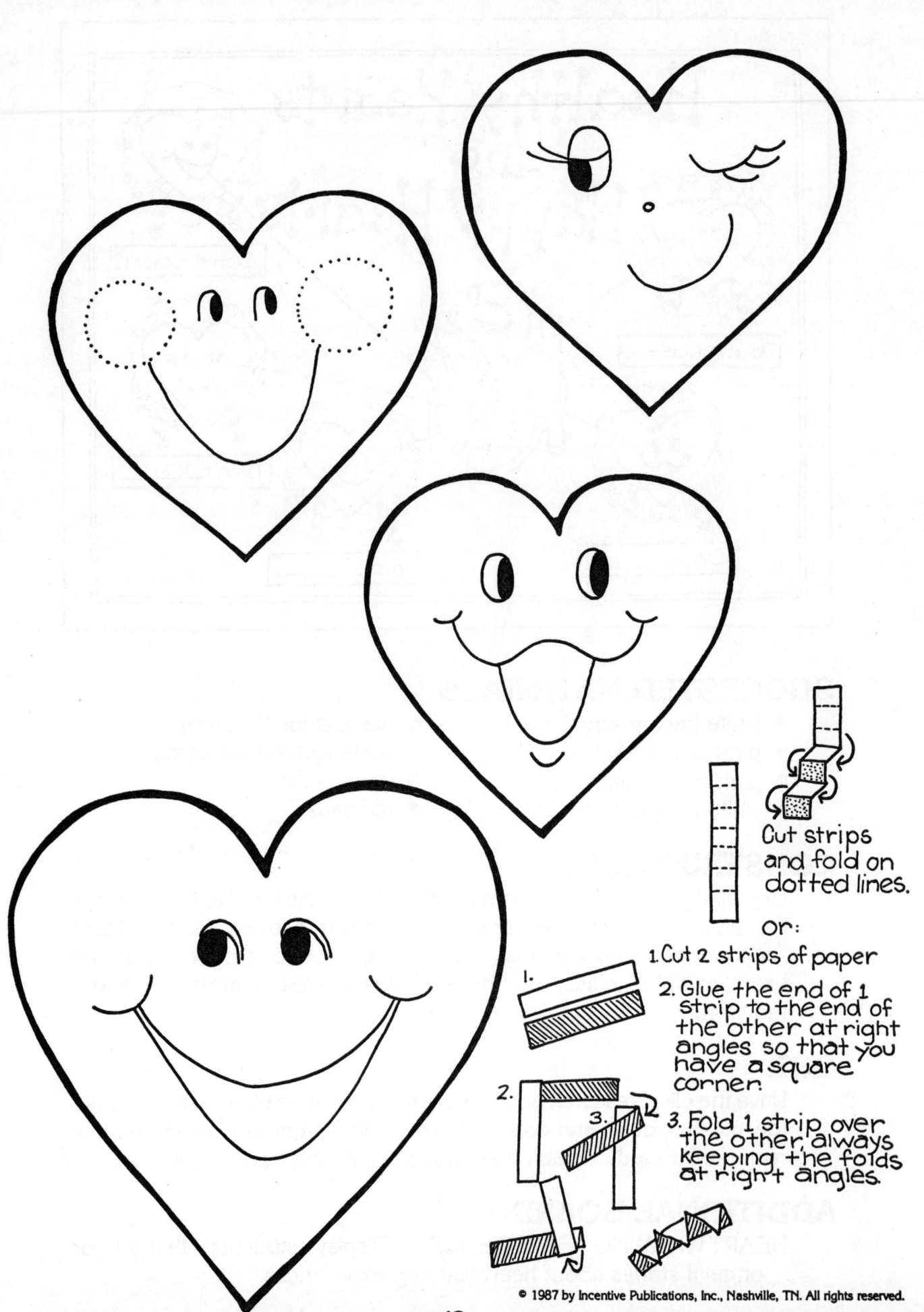

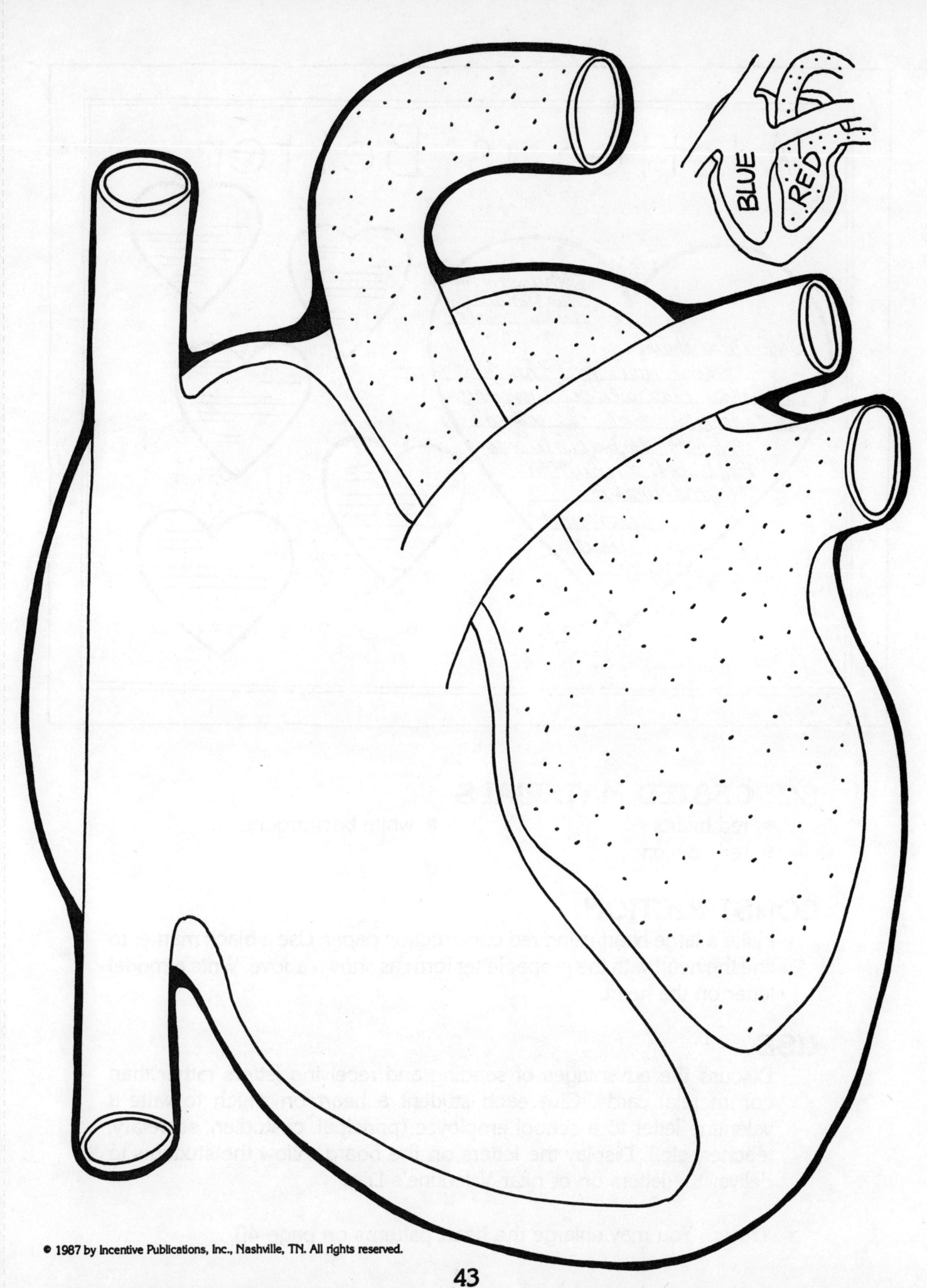

SUGGESTED MATERIALS
- red hearts
- red caption
- white background

CONSTRUCTION
Make a large heart using red construction paper. Use a black marker to line the heart with the proper letter form as shown above. Write a model letter on the heart.

USE
Discuss the advantages of sending and receiving letters rather than commercial cards. Give each student a heart on which to write a valentine letter to a school employee (principal, custodian, secretary, teacher, etc.). Display the letters on the board. Allow the students to deliver the letters on or near Valentine's Day.

Note: You may enlarge the heart patterns on page 40.

SUGGESTED MATERIALS
- light blue sky
- black caption
- dark blue water
- gray space capsule

CONSTRUCTION
Enlarge the space capsule and cut it out of gray construction paper. Decorate the capsule with markers.

USE
Have students write stories about what it would be like to travel in space. Display them on the board.

ADDITIONAL BOARDS
DREAMS BECOME REALITIES
SPLASH FLASH

Note: On February 20, 1962, John Glenn orbited the earth.

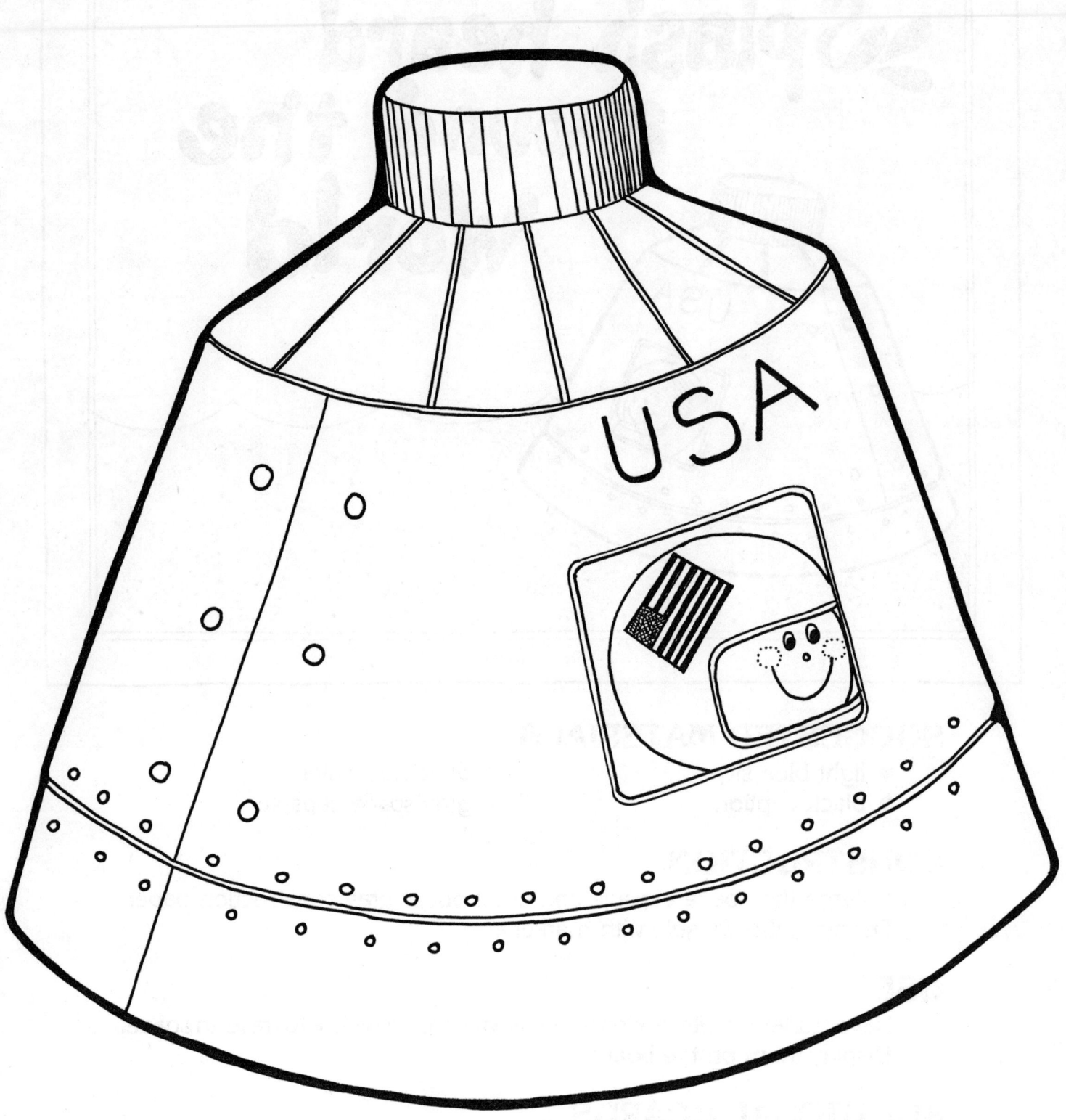

SUGGESTED MATERIALS
- blue background
- white caption
- white snowman
- green tree, brown trunk
- red sled
- yellow sun

CONSTRUCTION
Enlarge the pattern on page 18 and color it accordingly. Enlarge the melting snowman, sled, and boy patterns and color each with markers.

USE
Have students draw, paint, or construct paper illustrations of spring signs (birds, buds, insects, etc.). Display the work on the board. Add students' original stories or poems about spring.

You may cut a piece of yarn and thread through holes in sled bar for rope pull.

© 1987 by Incentive Publications, Inc., Nashville, TN. All rights reserved.

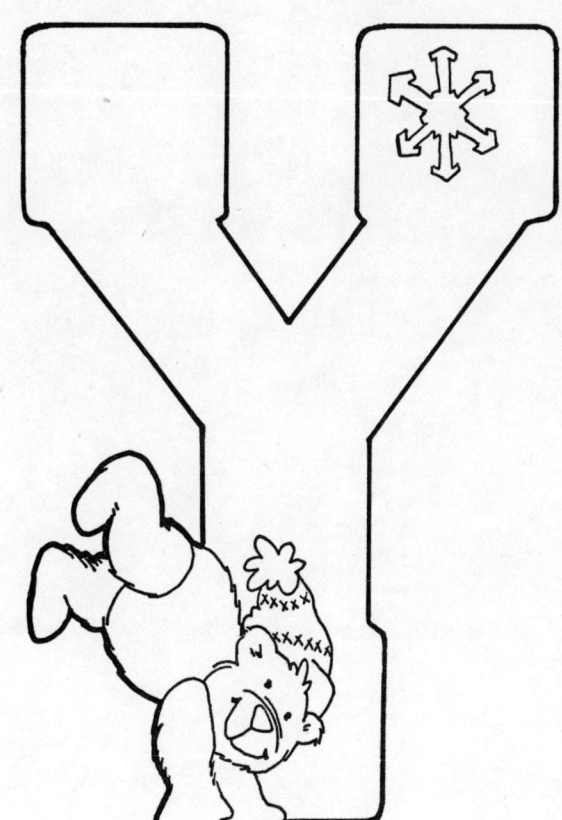